NATIONAL LIBRARY OF POCKET POETS

§ § § § §

BLUE OBOE

A Book of Poems

by

David Garrison

§ § § § §

WYNDHAM HALL PRESS

BLUE OBOE

A Book of Poems

by

David Garrison

Illustrations by David Leach

ISBN 0-932269-14-1

Printed in the United States of America

B L U E   O B O E

"The imagistic poems of David Garrison display a sharp eye, an admirable capacity to praise this world, and, best of all, startling and intelligent flourishes of real humor."

-- Jonathan Holden

"Blue Oboe combines exact and convincing scenes with a point of view that is sometimes humorous, sometimes nostalgic. The blend carries the reader on an excursion that feels like life, a vivid life with side-glances at family episodes, school-time experiences, and those transcending glimpses that deft language can bring."

-- William Stafford

ACKNOWLEDGMENTS

The author would like to acknowledge previous publication of the following poems and express his sincere appreciation to the editors of the journals in which they appeared: "Goodbye, Mr. Clark," "Covenant," "Birthday," "Otherness," in Modern Images; "November," "Sleeping in the Cosmos," in Manna; "Ich bin Gregor Samsa," in Orphic Lute; "The Unemployment Office," in The Cape Rock; "Chalkdust," in Denver Quarterly; "Metaphors for Dinner," in Gusto; "Reflections," in Poetry Today Supplement; "Hitler is Alive and Living in Ohio," "The True Meaning of High School," in Nexus; and "Cauldrons," in The New Poets Review, where it won Third Prize in the magazine's 1983 national contest.

for Dale, Inez, James, Glen, and Ann Garrison

and for Suzanne Kelly-Garrison

TABLE OF CONTENTS

FALL

BLUE OBOE

On that fall day round
and cool as a ripe apple,
when a blue oboe tunes the leaves,
the stream, the hillsides,
when lost threads of our lives
lie fertile and exposed
like pine needles,
we walk the forest.
You whistle to the birds
and fool them
with mating calls that end
in Irish ballads. The curve
of your hips sums up
the curves of tree and sky,
calling me home where
we play, in perfect tune,
apple, echoes, threads,
the warm dark core of love.

GOODBYE, MR. CLARK

He corrected exams on his wedding night,
sat toward the middle of his car seat
so the tires would wear evenly,
saved thousands of orange juice cans.
Those were the rumors.

Tall, salt and pepper whiskers,
forty years a French Teacher.
He smiled as if he didn't understand
the joke but wanted to be pleasant.
The children would answer him
in whispers until he leaned forward
and turned up his hearing aid,
then someone shouted so loud
he reared back in pain.
When the children would no longer
sit still for Latin and Greek roots,
a mandatory retirement age was invented
just for Mr. Clark. He muttered, refused
to sign and pass the memos.
On warm afternoons he would shuffle
out to the baseball diamond
and stand behind the backstop,
stretching his arms wide as he could
to clap when our team scored a run.
On the last day of school his students
piled chairs to the ceiling that fell
on him when he opened his classroom door.

HALLIE'S PLACE

(for Hallie Craytor)

The house is lush with the comfort
of books, porcelain figurines,
a thousand other tiny things,
each one in place.
A reproduction of God
touching Adam's finger
covers only half the ceiling stain
above this bright-eyed rascal
in her faded green rocker
who has told stories
for more than eighty years.
The hoarse voice of this woman
who cannot climb stairs
rocks me with stories up a winding
staircase to a snowfilled fir tree,
to the wax wings of a boy who fell
from grace, to untouched fruit,
to a last look back,
to the edge of a pond reflecting
the forgotten features of a lion.
The clock ticks steady darkness
as we drink our tea
inside the sound of rain.

NOVEMBER

Like black notes
on gray staves of oak and ash,
grackles gather.
Measure by measure
they lade the branches,
then swirl away in speckled clouds.

SLEEPING IN THE COSMOS

I chase sleep
through six constellations
until we glance off each other,
giggling like drunks
knocking heads.
The moon tugs me into orbit
on a band of blue light,
but I cannot hang on.
Clawing and sweating,
I crash to earth
inside my alarm clock.

MANNA

(near Redcliff, Colorado)

This mountain is a cold nest
for our campsite buried
in the shadow of pines
that hide half the sky
until morning slices through them
like gold hair through a comb.
When the sun is in the tent
we get out and start a fire.
We toast bread on long sticks,
tossing bits of it to chipmunks,
manna they accept as we accept
the smell of burning wood.
We should begin each day like this:
not feeling alone.

STILL LIFE

A red freight car stands
still on the siding, framed by
green leaves turning red.

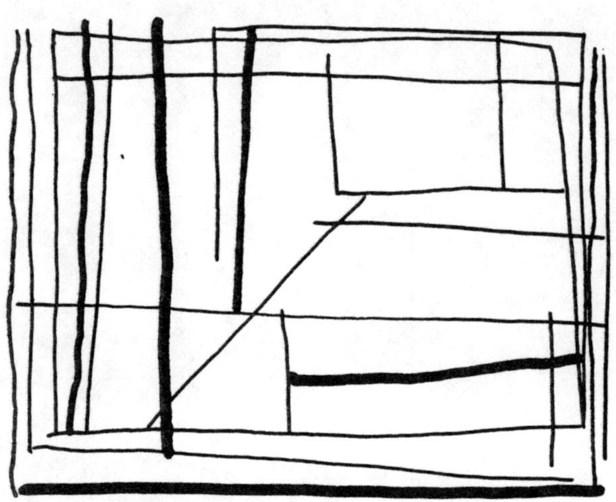

WINTER

CAULDRONS

Sleep draws us apart
as if opposing magnetic forces
pull us back
to that distant solitary darkness
where we boil our lives
in separate cauldrons,
snatching now and then
a blackened pun or riddle
to share at breakfast.

ICH BIN GREGOR SAMSA

"As Gregor Samsa awoke one morning from uneasy dreams he found himself transformed in his bed into a gigantic insect."

Franz Kafka, "The Metamorphosis"

The phone rings and I tell the life
insurance salesman my life
is whole already. I tell him
I have no wife or family to protect.
I tell him I am stinking rich.
I tell him I am Gregor Samsa
and may metamorphose at any minute.
I tell him a nuclear attack will
vaporize us all and only
the cockroaches will survive.
"Listen," I say, "I'm immortal,
immortal as a damned cockroach!"
"Well," he pauses, "we also offer
auto, fire, and homeowner policies."

HITLER IS ALIVE AND LIVING IN OHIO

Add the mustache,
slick down the hair,
choke with a tie,
raise the right·hand,
and yes, that's him.
It's the muscled arch
of the eyebrows,
the menacing dimples
that give him away.
He did escape, you know,
in a submarine to Ohio,
where he poisons us
like acid rain:
we can't forgive;
we conspire against love,
torture one another
and ourselves,
wallow in pettiness.
Sometimes I see
that mad smile of his
when I look closely
in the mirror.

THE UNEMPLOYMENT OFFICE

Heavy-bearded burly men
in denim jackets,
big-breasted women gabbing in low tones
over coffee, alert
to the edges of their children's play.
Neither employees nor unemployed
heed "No Smoking" signs
taped on the brown walls
above the ashtrays.
Brown linoleum floors,
brown tables, desks, and chairs.
The slamming of brown file cabinets
interrupts the white harmony
of snow sticking outside.
My name is called three times
before I recognize it.

FOG ON PUGET SOUND

Waves divide and subdivide
the moonlight, lapping blackness
against a rowboat
lashed to that empty pier.
A gray mass steals
through lines of evergreens,
sweeps across the water
and holds the bay, unyielding.

LISTEN, SWEETHEART

I want to watch "Casablanca"
on the late show
snuggled in bed with you
while the cat sleeps
against our tucked-together legs.

DESIRE

There is a piece of
coal deep inside me that wants
to be a diamond.

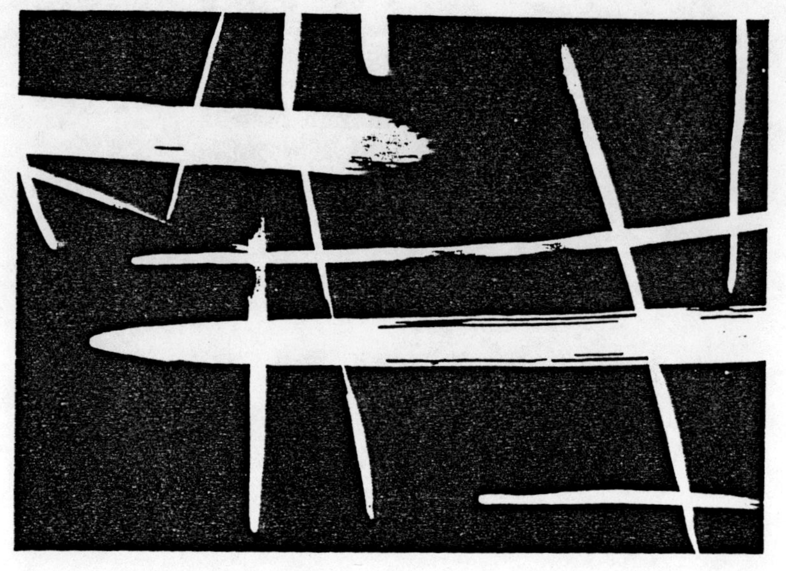

SPRING

CHALKDUST

Halfway through Dante
the professor looked out the window
and lost his way,
stood staring into the eyes
of the lithe leopard,
into five years of his pilgrimage
to tenure and nearly twelve
with chalkdust on his back.
Lost himself among the birds outside
that swooped and scattered
through the darkening churchyard.
"Go find the way," he said,
not turning back
to the startled, well-scrubbed faces.
He gazed until the sun
was blood on the hillside,
then quietly found his way
home through the churchyard
on one of those irreverent paths
the living make among the dead.

BIRTHDAY

In high school the coach reminded us
the other team's players put their pants on
one leg at a time.
This morning, newly arrived at age thirty-four,
I stumbled getting into the first leg,
fell on the bed and realized
why I never made the starting team.
All day I kept falling giddy
into memories, finding myself
in squeaking doors, a favorite pen,
dog-eared maps, and rain.
I heard a songbird somewhere
in the rippling layered dome of a tree
and walked three times around it
looking for my past.

OTHERNESS

Each night we touch and talk,
slowly learning the strange otherness
of each other.

METAPHORS FOR DINNER

Words stick to my imagination
like wet cucumber peelings to the sink.
The mind is a salad of words
cut from the garden of experience
and death is the great disposal of verbiage.
When my wife--a real tomato--
asks "What kind of smile is that?"
I wink and tell her
I'm mixing some metaphors for dinner.

COVENANT

With the red and gold
of its wings the blackbird
draws rainbows on the blue air.
In each swift arc it renews
its covenant with earth and us.

THE TRUE MEANING OF HIGH SCHOOL

I locked myself into a lavatory stall
to count my pictures in the yearbook,
forgot to breathe
until it was clear that with fourteen
I tied for Most Pictured Senior.
I stayed home sick
the day they photographed the French Club
or I would have won.

EPITAPH

His necktie strangled,
dragged him day by dying day
to a tight coffin.

SUMMER

DREAM

A night train carried me
back to another home
closer to the tracks,
where I used to walk the rails,
examine sleeked metal,
splintered wear and tear
drummed into ties,
back to slow, full-moon
summer nights spent counting
freight cars at the trestle,
back to a trainride across dark
loam in steady, fertile winds
and silver watertowers, back to
a boy, sitting beside his mother,
staring out a window that framed
the brown slippery body
of the Mississippi,
spelling the river's name
over and over and over
to the blind rhythm of the train.

TO THE SHORE

On hot days we pedaled our bikes down
the melting asphalt road over that steep
hill of blackberry bushes and scotch broom

right into the cold foam of the bay.
Then we gathered smooth flat stones
and skipped them. A good one, polished

by a million or a billion years of sea
and sand, would hop ten times before
it sank. I walked down that hill

to the beach one night years later
and cried for the passing of my life.
Amid the dark patience of rock and water

I watched waves sweep stones to the shore
and suck them back in deep salty breaths.

REFLECTIONS

(for my parents)

We jump from rock to rock
down the cove's black ledges
to watch our children swim.
The sunlit water swells
against the bank, flashing
and distorting their limbs
beneath the surface. We drink
long and deep of them,
and ponder our reflections
in green tidepools.

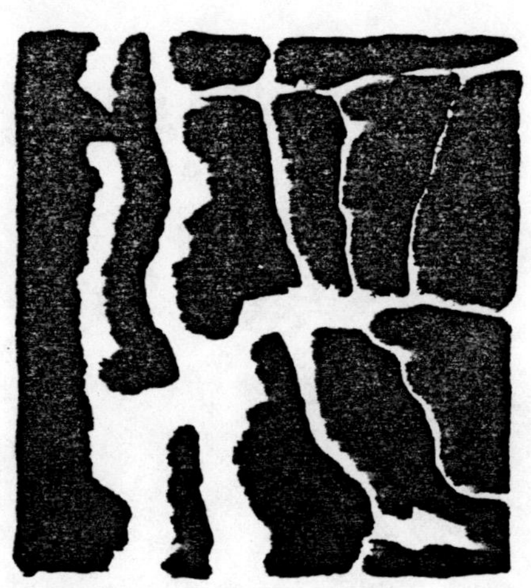

THE POET'S WIFE RESORTS TO SARCASM

Our bodies still coupled
but cooling,
I tell her there's a sale
on lawn furniture
at the discount store.
Cooling fast now,
she tells me
"that's a poetic thing to say
at a time like this.
You're a cross
between John Donne and Ogden Nash."

HOUSE FOR SALE

She opens the door and cats fall out
as if they'd been stacked
three feet high against it.
Cats curled in living room chairs
below reproductions of cats
and matadors, cats on top
of the refrigerator like ceramic statues,
cats pawing each other on the beds,
cats underfoot in the stairways,
cats squatting in boxes everywhere;
my eyes itch and I'm holding my breath.
Two cats tend their litters in the basement,
where she pauses, picks up
a handful of feline and says,
"I'd like to give some kittens away,
but you can't be too careful
these days. So many people feed them
to their boa constrictors..."

THAT HOUR OF SPARROWS

when the earth is discovering itself,
when gray meets gray dawn
and becomes horizon.
Dogs stir and stretch,
children mumble in their sleep,
and knowing oneself
is knowing one's face in the mirror.
Before the first sip of coffee,
before the wind comes up
and spiders bind their prey,
before car engines ignite another day,
that pause, that long look out the window
at nothing in particular.

HAIKU

grass turns yellow
gray air lies down
before the summer rainstorm

too tired to talk
you sleep in your clothes
talk in your sleep

woodpecker drills me
awake with his monotone
makes me think of work

pumping high
in the swing at twilight
no regrets

spillway as full as
the moon tonight, mosquitoes
biting like walleye

ABOUT THE AUTHOR

David Garrison was born in Bremerton, Washington, in 1945. He received a B.A. from Wesleyan University, M.A. degrees from Catholic University and Indiana University, and a Ph.D. in Romance Languages from Johns Hopkins. Since 1979 he has been teaching Spanish, Portuguese, and Comparative Literature at Wright State University. His translations from Spanish have been published in various magazines and anthologies, and with Willis Barnstone he translated A Bird of Paper: Poems of Vicente Aleixandre (Ohio University Press). His original poems have appeared in Modern Images, The Cape Rock, Denver Quarterly, and several other journals. He lives with his wife, Suzanne Kelly-Garrison, in Beavercreek, Ohio.